IMAGES OF WAR

GERMAN SELF-PROPELLED ANTI-TANK AND ANTI-AIRCRAFT GUNS, 1939–45

RARE PHOTOGRAPHS FROM WARTIME ARCHIVES

Ian Baxter

Pen & Sword
MILITARY

First published in Great Britain in 2025 by
PEN & SWORD MILITARY
an imprint of Pen & Sword Books Ltd
Yorkshire – Philadelphia

ISBN 978-1-03610-060-5

A CIP catalogue record for this book is available from the British Library.

Typeset by Concept, Huddersfield, West Yorkshire, HD4 5JL
Printed and bound in England by CPI Group (UK) Ltd, Croydon, CR0 4YY

The Publisher's authorised representative in the EU for product safety is Authorised Rep Compliance Ltd, Ground Floor, 71 Lower Baggot Street, Dublin D02 P593, Ireland – www.arccompliance.com

For a complete list of Pen & Sword titles please contact
PEN & SWORD BOOKS LTD
47 Church Street, Barnsley, South Yorkshire, S70 2AS, England
E-mail: enquiries@pen-and-sword.co.uk
Website: www.pen-and-sword.co.uk
or
PEN & SWORD BOOKS
1950 Lawrence Road, Havertown, PA 19083, USA
E-mail: uspen-and-sword@casematepublishers.com
Website: www.penandswordbooks.com

Contents

About the Author

Ian Baxter is a military historian who specialises in German twentieth-century military history. He has written more than seventy books, including *Poland: The Eighteen-Day Victory March*; *Panzers in North Africa*; *The Waffen-SS Ardennes Offensive*; *The Western Campaign*; *The 12th SS Panzer Division Hitlerjugend*; *Waffen-SS on the Western Front*; *Waffen-SS on the Eastern Front*; *The Red Army at Stalingrad*; *Elite German Forces of World War II*; *Armoured Warfare: German Tanks of World War II*; *Blitzkrieg*; *Panzer Divisions at War*; *German Armoured Vehicles of World War Two*; *Last Two Years of the Waffen-SS at War*; *German Soldier Uniforms and Insignia*; *German Guns of the Third Reich*; *From Retreat to Defeat: The Last Years of the German Army at War 1943–45* and, most recently, *The Sixth Army and the Road to Stalingrad*.

He has written over a hundred articles, including 'Last days of Hitler', 'Wolf's Lair', 'The Story of the V1 and V2 Rocket Programme', 'Secret Aircraft of World War Two', 'Rommel at Tobruk', 'Hitler's War with his Generals', 'Secret British Plans to Assassinate Hitler', 'The SS at Arnhem', 'Hitlerjugend', 'Battle of Caen 1944', 'Gebirgsjäger at War', 'Panzer Crews', 'Hitlerjugend Guerrillas', 'Last Battles in the East', 'The Battle of Berlin' and many more.

He has also reviewed numerous military studies for publication, supplied thousands of photographs and important documents to various publishers and film production companies worldwide, and he lectures to schools, colleges and universities throughout the United Kingdom and Southern Ireland.

Introduction

This book tells the story of German anti-tank and anti-aircraft vehicles, which made their first appearance in 1939 as combatants developed effective armoured vehicles and tactics. Some were little more than stop-gap solutions, mounting anti-tank/anti-aircraft guns on a tracked vehicle to give mobility, while others were more sophisticated in design. Examples of the development of tank destroyer technology throughout the Second World War are the Marders, Jagdpanzer 38 and Nashorn. In order to provide much-needed firepower during the war, vehicles like the 5-ton Sd.Kfz.6 half-track mounted Soviet 76.2mm field guns. There was also the Marder series, which supported the armoured drive with anti-tank guns.

In addition, much-needed air support was vital to give protection to these vehicles and tanks in the field. For that reason, the Germans mounted anti-tank guns on board half-tracks, such as the Sd.Kfz.10/5 and 10/4 armed with 2cm Flak guns, and the medium Sd.Kfz.7/1 half-track mounting 2cm Flak guns, including quadruple Flak guns on certain modified vehicles. Later in the war, there was the Flakpanzer 38(t), which mounted a 2cm Flak gun, an Sd.Kfz.6/2 Flak half-track, and the Flakpanzer IV Wirbelwind (Whirlwind) with a rotating Flak gun turret armed with quadruple 2cm Flak guns.

Chapter One

A New Concept (1939–40)

Following Germany's swift victory over Poland in September 1939, the Panzerwaffe (German Armoured Force) highlighted the necessity to produce a tank destroyer, tank hunter or tank killer (Jagdpanzer). This armoured vehicle would typically be armed with a direct artillery gun, also known as a self-propelled gun. The vehicle would be specifically designed to engage and destroy enemy tanks. While operating on the front line it would support armoured troops and armoured fighting vehicles and be used for operational mobility, as well as having tactical offensive and defensive capabilities. These dedicated anti-tank vehicles would become an integral part of the Panzerwaffe and be effective on the battlefield. Mounting an anti-tank gun on a tracked vehicle would give these new machines good mobility and the capacity to be able to fight their way through enemy lines against tanks and other fighting vehicles.

Another vehicle that the Germans wanted to convert in their masses alongside the Jagdpanzer was the anti-aircraft gun (Flakpanzer). These specific vehicles' weapons were usually designed on a mounted quick-traversing turret with a high rate of elevation, for tracking fast-moving aircraft. They were also designed to be used against surface targets, which they did to great effect. Plans for these vehicles also incorporated dual or quadruple mounts, allowing a high rate of fire.

Following their victory in Poland, the Germans were well aware that the key to success against enemy vehicles would be utilising self-propelled anti-tank and anti-aircraft weaponry instead of towed guns. This would ensure that anti-tank and anti-aircraft batteries could reach the front lines quickly and do their job effectively. Operations in Poland had proved that moving towed ordnance by animal draught was antiquated and slow. Crews would choose a desired position to set up their gun, and then unlimber and prepare the weapon for a fire mission. After the gun had been fired at its target, the crew would then have to limber it back up and move slowly to another position. This process was hardly the German blitzkrieg doctrine, which had been formulated to win wars by using offensive warfare designed to strike a swift, focused blow at an enemy using mobile, manoeuvrable forces, including armoured tanks and air support. The only way that blitzkrieg could be achieved cohesively was to adopt self-propelled artillery vehicles in the field. Unlike towed artillery, these mounted gun vehicles could move rapidly, stop quickly, choose a location, and then begin firing almost immediately. They could then quickly move on to a new position. This fire-and-move ability would make mobile conflict particularly successful during an advance. The capabilities of self-propelled artillery also meant increased survivability for units fighting in the field.

Mobility on the battlefield was key to the success of the self-propelled artillery vehicles, but designers knew that success also depended on weight, speed, range and manoeuvrability. The tactical requirements that led to the design of self-propelled artillery vehicles emerged from the need to follow the panzer into action over long distances. These vehicles were conceived to achieve armour penetration and protect the skies at maximum ranges by using relatively heavy ammunition with high velocities. Their design and use would enable the Germans to gain tactical mobility. At a moment's notice, such a vehicle could halt, change direction and quickly fire at an enemy target. The German principle of attack was all about fast-moving and changing combat, and most of all, gaining supremacy of a given area quickly.

However, regardless of the ideas put forward by designers on mass-producing and adapting these vehicles into fast-moving, self-propelled artillery machines, both the Jagdpanzer and the Flakpanzer were almost completely overlooked by Germany when it invaded the Low Countries and France in May and June 1940. In spite of this, a new arsenal of self-propelled artillery machines did make their debuts alongside both the Wehrmacht and their Waffen-SS counterparts.

The first converted vehicle, introduced in May 1940, was known as the Panzerjäger I (tank hunter Mk I). It mounted a Czech 4.7cm KPUV vz. 38 gun, but was initially designated by the Germans as a 4.7cm PaK(t) (Sf.) auf Pz.Kpfw.I (Sd.Kfz.101) ohne Turm anti-tank gun, which was converted onto a Panzerkampfwagen I or Pz.Kpfw.I Ausf. B chassis. The vehicle was designed to counter heavy French tanks such as the Char B1 bis, which were beyond the capabilities of the 3.7cm PaK 35/36 anti-tank gun. The 3.7cm PaK was the main anti-tank gun used in the Wehrmacht's arsenal during operations in Poland, and it had proved very effective against Polish tanks and numerous other armoured vehicles. Hundreds of these weapons had been built for the Germans by the Škoda factory in Czechoslovakia. The standard round of this Panzergranate Pz.Gr.36(t) had a muzzle velocity of 775m/s and a maximum effective range of 1.5km. The armour penetration for a standard AP round was 48–59mm at 500m, and 41mm just under 1.6km. The weapon was capable of destroying most tanks at relatively long distance, apart from the French B1 or British Matilda. The gun could also fire high-explosive rounds with impact fuses, but these were broadly designed to be used against lighter tanks. Fortunately for the Germans, the majority of the enemy tanks that the troops would confront were generally lighter. The Panzergranate Pz.Gr.36(t) would prove inadequate against the heavier enemy tanks, with poor penetration, and this did cause some concern among some of the tacticians. While this anti-tank gun had done a satisfactory job on the battlefields of Poland, the Germans were aware they needed more powerful guns, with strong anti-tank capabilities. The 5cm PaK 38 would have been the most effective gun in combating heavier French vehicles, but during the early summer of 1940, the weapon was still in development. Instead, the Heereswaffenamt (HWA, ordnance department) proposed mounting the Czech 4.7cm PaK gun onto a modified Pz.Kpfw.I Ausf. B tank chassis. However, the HWA was eager to give the first Panzerjäger a better edge on the battlefield and a proposal to use the Pz.Kpf.II was put forward. Even the Pz.Kpfw.III was considered, but the Panzerwaffe regarded this model as too important and scarce for a conversion. Instead, Altmärkische Kettenfabrik (Alkett), a Berlin manufacturer, designed and built the first Panzerjäger. Some 132 vehicles were given to Alkett in early 1940 and these were to be converted in preparation for the attack against the West. The Ausf. B variant was chosen as it had a more powerful engine than the Ausf. A. Its engine was a water-cooled 100hp 3.8 litre Maybach NL 38 TR. Due to its conversion, the weight of the machine was increased to 6.4 tonnes, which hindered the handling of the vehicle and cross-road performance. The Panzerjäger could only manage a maximum speed of almost 25mph.

During the vehicle's modification at the factory, the tank turret was removed along with the upper and rear armour. The 4.7cm gun was then lowered onto the chassis where the turret was once installed and the gun mount bolted in place by special metal bars. A gun shield was also installed, and the first series of these vehicles included a five-sided armoured compartment in order to protect the crew.

The total ammunition load of the vehicle carried eighty-six rounds, which were contained in five ammunition boxes. The three-man crew were also given adequate radio equipment and provided with the Fu 2 receiver. Space on board these vehicles was very cramped. The driver was located inside the vehicle, along with the radio operator. The commander, who was also the gunner, was positioned on the left side of the armoured compartment. The loader was located next to the commander, on the right-hand side.

For operations against the West, the Panzerjäger I was used to equip the Panzerjäger-Abteilung (Pz.Jg.Abt.), anti-tank battalions, using guns on self-propelled carriages. Each component of the Pz.Jg.Abt. comprised one Stab

Pz.Jg.Abt., equipped with one Panzer I Ausf. B, and three companies. Each of these companies was equipped with nine vehicles. The companies were divided into platoons. Each platoon comprised three vehicles and one Sd.Kfz.10 half-track for ammunition supply.

In preparation for the invasion against the West, it was planned that four anti-battalions would be used, but by 10 May 1940, only Pz.Jg.Abt. 521 was combat ready, with eighteen vehicles, six in each company. The other battalions, comprising the 616th, 643rd and 670th, were still being prepared for front-line operations, but would eventually see action in the West. In total, twenty-seven vehicles were being equipped in each of these new battalions.

As for Pz.Jg.Abt. 521, it was allocated under Panzergruppe Kleist 1st Panzer Army. Panzergruppe Kleist played a significant role in the Battle of Belgium (10–28 May 1940), where it drove its forces through the Ardennes and then swung north-west towards the sea. Its wide-sweeping advance created a huge pocket containing a number of Belgian, British and French armies.

Operations in Belgium and then in France saw the Panzerjäger I become a very successful fighting machine, using its 4.7cm gun with great effect. During battle, it was able to penetrate the majority of Allied tanks and knock them out from ranges as far as 500 to 600 metres. The tank hunter was also effective at knocking out various lines of defences, including machine-gun nests and other related targets.

Throughout the Battle of France (otherwise known as the Western Campaign, 10 May–25 June 1940), the strategic onus of ground movement lay totally with armour, and troops relied almost invariably upon it. The consequence was that the best-armoured formations had to thrust forward repeatedly into the heart of the battle. Losses were therefore inevitable. However, French tactics proved to be not only unimaginative, but also unable to cope with the rapid speed with which events were unfolding. There was nothing cowardly about the performance of the French Army, but they were simply overwhelmed by the German tactics of blitzkrieg. Faced with the total collapse of their army, they continued to display sacrificial courage.

By late June 1940, the Battle of France ended with another victory for the Germans. They had reaped the rewards of another dramatic blitzkrieg campaign. France had proven ideal tank country in which to undertake a lightening war, and its conception seemed flawless. To many of the tacticians, blitzkrieg would ensure future victories.

As for the Panzerjäger, operations in the West had equally proven successful. Its tactics had been tried and tested and many of the Allied tanks it fought against were knocked out of action as a result of its 4.7cm gun. However, in spite of its success as the first tank hunter in the German arsenal there were a number of problems with the machine. Although it was highly mobile on the battlefield compared to towed anti-tank guns, the vehicle was prone to various mechanical problems. Some vehicles developed suspension problems whilst others overheated. Also, the lack of proper telescopic sights for observation made operating the 'hunter' perilously dangerous for the crew. As a result, the commander frequently had to rely on the gun sight, and this often made navigating the vehicle on the battlefield while it was on the move very problematic. Armour protection was also very minimal and its main 13mm armour provided limited protection against heavier Allied tanks. The open-top crew compartment proved dangerous, too. Although the armoured shield was slightly thicker at 14.5mm, the crew were often open to hostile fire and as a result, were shot by small arms fire. The crew compartment was also very small and lacked sufficient space for additional equipment or personal belongings. Although a stowage bin had been bolted on the right fender for additional gear, it still proved inadequate.

Despite the mechanical problems and design issues of the Panzerjäger I, the vehicle proved valuable in 1940 and was an integral part of the blitzkrieg success. But it was not just the new tank hunter that made its debut in 1940; self-propelled anti-aircraft guns, or Flakpanzers, were seen supporting the advance through the Low Countries and France. The Sd.Kfz.10, or Sonderkraftfahrzeug (special motorised vehicle), was a German half-track that saw extensive operations during the war. It was chiefly built as a prime mover designed to tow small ordnance such as the 2cm Flak 30, 7.5cm le.IG, or the 3.7cm PaK 36 anti-tank gun. The concept of using self-propelled Flak guns was agreed before the invasion of Poland. In fact, although very few in number and most of which never saw much aerial action, there were Sd.Kfz.10/4 half-tracks that were operational in Poland with mounted Flak guns. These vehicles were allocated to support five panzer divisions, four light divisions, and four motorised infantry divisions. Then the Flak 30 gun had to be mounted manually onto the platform on the rear of the vehicle without any support. The rear of the half-track, which previously provided storage space, was reinforced to make it strong enough to support the weight of a gun, the crew and other equipment. Initially, the gun had to be loaded on top of the vehicle with the assistance of two ramps. This was an interim solution and hardly practical for the crew if they were required to move quickly from one position on the front to another. There was also no gun shield, and this left the gun crew totally exposed to enemy fire. However, following the invasion of Poland it was agreed that the Sd.Kfz.10 was versatile enough in its design to accommodate a self-propelled Flak gun, which was permanently bolted to the rear of the chassis and able to traverse and fire at enemy targets.

By 1940, there were numerous variants of the Sd.Kfz.10 half-track built and assigned for various roles on the battlefield. Because of the unique design of the half-track, the Sd.Kfz.10/4 and Sd.Kfz.10/5 were converted into Flak vehicles, complete with a 2cm Flak 30 mounted on a special platform on the rear, with fold-down side and rear panels to allow room for the crew of six or seven to operate. Some of these vehicles had gun shields fitted, but it would not be until after operations in the West that all vehicles had to be built and operated with gun shields. Bolted to the side and rear panels were ammunition bins containing one twenty-round magazine each.

For operations against both Poland and the Western allies, all Sd.Kfz.10/4s were registered with the Luftwaffe and were attached to a panzer or infantry division. These half-tracks were all organised into leichte Flak-Abteilungen (Sf.), or light self-propelled anti-aircraft battalions. When attached to the army, they were renamed Heeres Flak-Battailone, or army anti-air battalions. A total of thirty-six Sd.Kfz.10/4s were distributed in three anti-aircraft platoons, with four Sd.Kfz.10/4s in each platoon.

During the invasion against the West, the Sd.Kfz.10/4 proved very successful, providing protection against air targets for the advancing tank divisions. Its performance was so good that it was also used against ground targets, and was regarded as more successful than the Pz.Kpfw. II, which was also armed with the 2cm gun.

Another half-track to be converted for operations in Poland, on the Western Front and during the early part of the invasion of Russia was the Sd.Kfz.8. It was designated as the 8.8cm Flak 18 (Sf.) auf Zugkraftwagen 12t (Sd.Kfz.8). A total of ten of these half-tracks were modified, comprising a mounted 8.8cm Flak 18 gun bolted on a pedestal on the rear of the artillery tractor. There was a gun shield to protect the crew. The driver's compartment was replaced by a lower, armoured cupola and the engine compartment was slightly strengthened. The Flak vehicles were rare and only ten saw operation, where they were assigned to the first company of the anti-tank battalion Panzerjäger-Abteilung 8.

(**Opposite, above**) A 4.7cm PaK Sf auf Panzerkampfwagen I Panzerjäger operating in France in 1940. During the German invasion of Poland in September 1939, the 3.7cm PaK 36 had been the main anti-tank gun. It had been very successful against Polish tanks and other armoured vehicles. However, Poland highlighted the necessity to produce a tank destroyer, tank hunter or tank killer (Jagdpanzer). It was therefore decided to mount the Czech 4.7cm gun on a modified Pz.Kpfw.I Ausf. B tank chassis.

(**Opposite, below**) A Panzerkampfwagen I Panzerjäger advances along a road in France. During the invasion of France, the Panzerjäger I would prove very effective on the battlefield and its 4.7cm gun was more than capable of knocking out most Allied tanks from over 500m. However, the machine was plagued with numerous mechanical issues.

An Sd.Kfz.10/4 operating in Donchery, in the Ardennes, France, next to the river Maas. This converted half-track mounts a Flak 30, which was developed as a light self-propelled anti-aircraft gun. Production of this vehicle began in 1939. The rifle mountings on the front mudguards were first fitted in 1940.

A Luftwaffe Sd.Kfz.7/2 3.7cm Flak 36 half-track advances through a French town.

A stationary 8.8cm Flak 18 (Sf.) auf schwerer Zugkraftwagen 12t (Sd.Kfz.8). These vehicles, mounting an 8.8cm Flak gun, were assigned to the first company of the anti-tank battalion Panzerjäger-Abteilung 8, which participated in the invasion of Poland in 1939, France in 1940, and later, during the early part of the invasion of Russian in 1941. Note the camouflage netting over the gun shield, and foliage attached.

An 8.8cm Flak 18 (Sf.) auf Zugkraftwagen 12t Sd.Kfz.8 half-track during operations in France in 1940. This vehicle was very effective at knocking out fortifications and various other bunker installations. However, its main role on the battlefield was in an anti-tank role.

An 8.8cm Flak 18 (Sf.) auf Zugkraftwagen 12t Sd.Kfz.8 half-track has been brought up to confront an enemy defensive line in France. The vehicle has halted and troops can be seen observing positions along the road before the half-track goes into action.

An Sd.Kfz.10/4 moves across country with foliage attached to break up its distinctive shape from both enemy ground and aerial observation. The crew are riding on the half-track's platform and it is evident from the photograph that space was a premium. Note the Sd.Ah.51 ammunition trailer on tow.

An excellent photograph showing a stationary Sd.Kfz.10/4 inside a French town. The vehicle's platform was specially designed to accommodate the 2cm Flak 30 gun.

Two Sd.Kfz.10/5 half-tracks can be seen advancing through a French town. Although this half-track provided troops with adequate cover against enemy aerial attacks, the vehicle also supported Wehrmacht and Waffen-SS forces with effective ground support.

A 2cm Flak 30 Sd.Kfz.10/4 advances through a field. Note the ammunition bins fastened to the sides. Each bin contained a single twenty-round magazine.

Chapter Two

Russia: First Generation (1941–43)

Following the victory over France in June 1940, the Germans captured a variety of both British and French armoured vehicles. Astonishingly, some 800 French Renault R35 tanks were captured. Through the course of 1940, the Inspectorate for Motorised and Armoured Units issued a report for the development of these captured vehicles and for modifying them into tank hunters. The R35 tank turret was removed and the 4.7cm Panzerabwehr-kanone 36(t), or 4.7cm PaK(t) cannon was mounted in its place, complete with the obsolete Pz.Kpfw.I chassis. Although the vehicle had a three-side shield that was poorly protected, the new 4.7cm PaK(t) (Sf.) auf Fgst. Pz.Kpfw.35R 731(f) was better built and stronger than the Panzerjäger I. By March 1941, the design of the vehicle was approved and an order for 200 of them was placed.

These vehicles first saw action on the Eastern Front and were used to form three thirty-vehicle, self-propelled anti-tank battalions that comprised the 559th, 561st and 611th. Each company was divided into small, three-vehicle platoons, complete with a reserve and training unit. However, their service in Russia was hampered by mechanical problems. In fact, the 611th Battalion lost all of its vehicles in the first day of the invasion due to either enemy fire or breakdown. The 559th Battalion also lost the majority of its machines.

Yet, in spite the significant loss of the new R35 tank hunter, operations on the Eastern Front during the summer of 1941 were a complete success for the Panzerwaffe. The panzer divisions had exploited the terrain and concerted such a series of hammer blows to the Red Army that commanders thought it was only a matter of time before the campaign would be over. Notwith-standing these successes, the panzer divisions were thinly spread. Although the armoured spearheads were still achieving rapid victories on all fronts, supporting units were not keeping pace with them. Consequently, it became increasingly difficult to keep armour supplied with fuel – and without fuel, the drive would grind to a halt. Nevertheless, between June and late September 1941, the Panzerwaffe were more or less unhindered by lack of supply, difficult terrain or bad weather conditions. However, on 6 October, the first snowfall of the approaching winter was reported. It melted quickly, but turned the dirt roads into quagmires and rivers into raging torrents. The Russian autumn, with its heavy rain, sleet and snow, had arrived. German armour began to slow. Wheeled vehicles soon became stuck in a sea of mud and could only advance with the aid of tracked vehicles towing them. No preparations had been made for the winter and German vehicles lacked the most basic supplies for cold weather. By the end of 1941, the battle-weary divisions of the Panzerwaffe, which had taken part in Operation Barbarossa, were no longer fit to fight. Mobile operations had consequently ground to a halt. Fortunately for the exhausted panzer crews and supporting units, no mobile operations had been planned for the winter of 1941/2.

In spite of the terrible problems that faced the badly depleted panzer divisions, back in Germany, the production of tanks, anti-tank and anti-aircraft vehicles continued to increase dramatically. In order to overcome the mammoth task of defeating the Red Army, more panzer divisions were being raised and motorised divisions were being converted into Panzergrenadier divisions. Although equipping the Panzerwaffe was a slow and expensive process, it was undertaken effectively, with the introduction of a number of new divisions being deployed on the front lines.

Supporting these new divisions, the Germans had been quickly developing new towed anti-tank guns such as the PaK 40, which was introduced in 1942. A much more powerful and potent PaK 43 would be introduced in 1943. By the spring of 1942, the Germans were already encountering never-ending numbers of Russian tanks. The battlefield was very fluid and movement was key to securing ground as quickly as possible. A way of overcoming this problem of mobility was once again to mount these new anti-tank guns on a tank chassis. As with previous designs, the vehicles were all to be open-topped, with limited traverse and inadequate armour protection. They would all be mounted with a potent anti-tank gun that would be easy to build and they would arrive on the battlefield in far greater numbers than ever before.

One of the potent weapons to be mounted on a tank was the Flak 41, which had seen widespread success on the battlefield on both the Western Front and the Eastern Front. The Germans looked at this as a temporary solution, but needed a vehicle capable of carrying the gun and engaging enemy tanks successfully.

In the summer of 1942, a new anti-tank gun was developed based on the 8.8cm Flak 41. Two companies – Krupp and Rheinmetall – were tasked with manufacturing and developing the machine. During the course of the second half of 1942, as fighting further intensified on the Eastern Front and the Battle of Stalingrad raged in southern Russia, developers were building the new self-propelled anti-tank vehicle, which was designated initially as the Sf. auf Pz.Kpfw.III/IV Fahrgestell Hornisse mitt 8.8cm PaK 43. There were also variations of different designations for this particular model through 1943, but Hitler himself would later change the name of Hornisse (Hornet) to Nashorn (Rhinoceros). The design of the machine was based on a modified Pz.Kpfw.III and IV tank chassis. The new chassis was actually designed and developed to be modified and converted for two different projects, one armed with the 8.8cm gun and the other with the 15cm s.F.H. 43 artillery gun. The 8.8cm Nashorn was built combining the designs of the Pz.Kpfw.III and IV. There were significant modifications to the vehicle. The engine compartment of the Pz.Kpfw.IV, for instance, was moved to the centre of the vehicle in order to allow sufficient room for the crew to operate the gun and avoid overheating. However, during its operational service, the vehicle continued to overheat, and it was a problem that was never really solved.

The design of the Nashorn, in spite of its potent gun and heavier, powerful converted tank, was similar to that of the very first Panzerjäger I. It had well-angled and basic armoured plates installed. The driver compartment on the left side was completely protected and the crew were also protected by armoured slats, but it was open from the top. To the rear of the vehicle, two doors allowed the crew access to enter the compartment. The whole vehicle was of basic design but the manufacturer had purposely kept the armour light for mobility. The introduction of the Nashorn in 1943 was still seen as a temporary solution and mass production of the vehicle was never intended, but as the war on the Eastern Front continued, there was a steady increase in manufacture.

The Nashorn had a crew of five, which comprised the commander, gunner, loader, driver and operator. The driver and operator were positioned in the front of the hull and were fully protected. Behind them, in the open combat compartment, were the rest of the crew. The gunner was positioned to the left of the gunner and behind him was the loader.

On the battlefield, it was planned that the Nashorn was planned be used to equip the Panzerjäger-Abteilung of the panzer divisions. However, this never happened and instead the vehicles were given to independent heavy anti-tank battalions. A number of these anti-tank battalions would be formed, comprising the Schwere Panzerjäger-Abteilung 88, 93, 424, 519, 525, 560, 655 and 664. Smaller units supplemented these battalions.

Production of the Nashorn was very slow; only six vehicles were received in February 1943 and an additional twenty-four in March. The factory was pressured into producing more of these vehicles quickly in preparation for the Kursk offensive, which was launched in July of that year.

In battle, the Nashorn was a very capable self-propelled anti-tank gun and could easily engage any Russian tank at significant ranges. The vehicle was able to support and increase the offensive capabilities with an effective anti-tank gun. But with the high armoured loss rate on the battlefield, these vehicles were required to help prop up the disintegrating front line and were often used as a main battle tank. As a result, losses were high. Also due to its weak armour, the vehicle could only provide limited protection; as a result, they could be easily destroyed by enemy fire. The Nashorn was not easily concealed and also suffered from ammunition supply problems, coupled with a small traverse arc. In addition, a number of them were prone to mechanical breakdown and overheating.

In spite of its problems, the Nashorn fought well, especially on the Eastern Front. However, armoured crews still found that their forces were increasingly vulnerable to Soviet counter-thrusts. Along the thinly stretched lines, crews often called for more mobile anti-tank firepower. As a result, the Germans were forced to develop further vehicles from various tank chassis. One vehicle that was heavily modified was known as the 10.5cm K gepanzerte Selbstfahrlafette (10.5cm gun on armoured self-propelled mount), also known as the Panzer Selbstfahrlafette IV Ausf. A (Pz.Sf. IVa) (Self-propelled anti-tank gun IV model A). It was a prototype self-propelled gun and although initially built in 1940 as a 'bunker buster', it was used on the Eastern Front as a tank destroyer. The vehicle mounted a powerful 10.5cm K gun, and was nicknamed the 'Dicker Max' (Thick or Fat Max). Two prototypes were assigned to Panzerjäger-Abteilung 521, but one caught fire and was completely destroyed. The other vehicle fought successfully until the end of 1941. In early 1942, the vehicle was completely modified and rebuilt and was then transported to southern Russia with the 521st. It was probably knocked out of action later that year as operational reports on the vehicle ceased by that period.

During 1942, other vehicles were modified and a new line, known as the Marder series, made their debut. These vehicles were relegated light tanks that were converted into tank hunters. The first Marder to be built was known as the 7.5cm PaK 40 auf Sf. Lorraine Schlepper 'Marder I' (Sd.Kfz.135). The vehicle was converted by adapting captured French Lorraine 37L fully tracked armoured tractors and mounting a German 7.5cm PaK 40 anti-tank gun. Once again, the design of this tank hunter followed the same construction methods used for other Panzerjäger. It was open-topped, with thin armour and the 7.5cm PaK 40/1 L/46 gun had limited traverse. However, the vehicle was very cheap to produce and a stopgap solution in combating the growing numbers of enemy tanks. On the battlefield, the Marder I was mostly incorporated in anti-tank battalions of infantry and some panzer divisions. In combat, these vehicles were seen fighting mostly on the Eastern Front and in France, and some were used in North Africa.

The Marder I made its debut in the summer of 1942. The 31st Infantry Division was reinforced with the vehicle while operating on the Eastern Front. However, due to overwhelming Russian resistance, most of the Marder Is were lost in battle. Only three remained by the end of October 1943, and they were given to Pz.Jg.Abt. 743 (Panzerjäger-Abteilung). By the beginning of 1944, none of the machines were operational.

Despite the losses in Russia, the majority of the newly built Marder Is were stationed in France. At a moment's notice they could be allocated to other fronts and supplied to both infantry and panzer divisions. The vehicles would see extensive action during the Allied Normandy landings in June 1944.

The Marder I, despite its high loss in Russia, was another drastic attempt by the Germans to solve the issue of towing anti-tank guns into battle by successfully converting the weapon into an effective mobile anti-tank gun vehicle. Due to the success of being able to convert the vehicles from obsolete tank chassis quickly and getting them onto the battlefield, the Germans produced another generation of Marder, known as the Marder II, which was produced in two versions. The first version was converted on light Pz.Kpfw.II Ausf. D/E and Flammpanzer II chassis. In the early part of the war, the Pz.Kpfw.II was regarded as the backbone of the Panzerwaffe, but by 1942 it was outdated, under-gunned and obsolete. The Germans therefore decided to convert the tank into the Marder II. The modification of the vehicle was simple. The upper superstructure and the tank turret were removed and in its place an anti-tank gun was mounted complete with a three-sided shield.

The first anti-tank gun used was a captured Russian 7.62cm gun, which was modified to accept the larger German 7.5cm PaK 40 propellant cartridge. On 1 April 1942, it was initially designated as the 7.62cm PaK 36(r) auf Fgst. Pz.Kpfw.II(F) (Sf.). However, two-months later it was renamed the Pz.Sf.1 fuer 7.62cm PaK 36 (Sd.Kfz.132). Further designations followed, but the machine remained generally unchanged.

The second version of the Marder II was known as the Panzerkampfwagen II als Sf. mit 7.5cm PaK 40 'Marder II' (Sd.Kfz.131). The tank hunter was based on a modified Pz.Kpfw.II Ausf. F tank chassis. Its design consisted of converting the tank and mounting a PaK 40 on the tank chassis. Production of these vehicles began at the same time as the first version of the Marder II.

Both versions of the Marder II were used to equip infantry and panzer divisions, and were seen operating in both Wehrmacht and Waffen-SS anti-tank companies. The vehicles were used mainly on the Eastern Front, and the majority were sent to southern Russia during the summer of 1942, where many of them were lost in battle. During operations in July 1943, the bulk of the Sd.Kfz.131 versions were used at Kursk, although many were lost.

The third version of Marder to see action on the Eastern Front was known as the Panzerjäger 38(t) für 7.62cm PaK 36(r) 'Marder III' (Sd.Kfz.139). Once again, the Germans used obsolete tank chassis, this time utilising the Pz.Kpfw.38(t) tank. The design involved removing the under-gunned 3.7cm KwK 38(t) gun and turret and replacing it with the Soviet 7.62cm PaK 36(r). Manufacturing of the Panzerjäger 38(t) Marder III commenced at the end of March 1942 and within weeks, the vehicle saw its debut with the Wehrmacht and Waffen-SS on the Eastern Front. Crews soon reported its tactical worth, as it was more than capable of destroying Soviet T-34 tanks. These tank hunters served extensively with the divisional anti-tank battalions and proved very successful at countering Russian armour. Between 1942 and 1944, some 1,500 Marder IIIs were produced.

While the Marder III was serving in the anti-tank battalions, some of the remaining 38(t) tank chassis were modified into self-propelled anti-aircraft gun vehicles. This new Flakpanzer, designated the Panzerkampfwagen 38 für 2cm Flak 38 (Sd.Kfz.140) Ausf. L Flakpanzer 38(t), was produced from 1943 to February 1944. The Flakpanzer 38(t) was modified using the standard Marder III Ausf. M variant. Its main armament consisted of a 2cm Flak 38 anti-aircraft cannon. The gun was introduced in order to phase out the older 2cm Flak 30, which was used extensively on Sd.Kfz.4 and Sd.Kfz.5 half-tracks throughout the war. The 2cm Flak 38 was also adapted as a mobile anti-aircraft weapon on the Sd.Kfz.4 and Sd.Kfz.5 half-tracks.

The 2cm Flak 38 proved a very capable weapon and the Flakpanzer 38(t) saw limited operations in Russia. The vehicles were organised into anti-aircraft tank platoons, each one comprising twelve vehicles. These were mainly incorporated into both Wehrmacht and Waffen-SS panzer divisions.

In a workshop are two 4.7cm PaK Pz.Kpfw.R35-731f. These vehicles were modified using a French Renault R35 and converted into a tank destroyer. The R35 was designed to support advancing troops, and with good firepower and mobility during the early part of the war on the Eastern Front in 1941, it was relatively successful.

A 4.7cm PaK Pz.Kpfw.R35 being transported on a trailer to the front during operations in Russia in the summer of 1941.

A motorcycle follows a column of 4.7cm PaK Pz.Kpfw.R35s operating on the Eastern Front. These vehicles were used to equip the German tank battalions and were allocated to individual infantry divisions to assist them in undertaking various offensive operations.

A Panzerkampfwagen I Panzerjäger belonging to Abteilung 616, pictured during a lull in operations in the summer of 1941 on the Eastern Front. By this period of the war, these tank hunters were no match against the growing Russian armour.

A Panzerjäger I operating with a panzer division in Russia. Initially, when this vehicle made its debut in France in 1940, it had been an integral part of the blitzkrieg success. However, in Russia, this tank hunter was outdated against more powerful Russian armour.

A half-track with mounted Flak gun belonging to the Waffen-SS Leibstandarte during operations in Russia in 1941.

A converted Sd.Kfz.7/1 mounting the powerful 2cm Flakvierling 38 quadruple Flak gun. The Flakvierling four-autocannon, anti-aircraft ordnance system was a very effective weapon and was used in a dual role against both air and ground targets.

A battery of Waffen-SS half-tracks with mounted Flak guns cover ground forces in an aerial role.

A 4.7cm PaK Pz.Kpfw.R35 during training in 1941. When these vehicles began their attack against the Red Army on the Eastern Front, within a day, the majority of these Panzerjäger were out of action due to mechanical breakdown.

An Sd.Kfz.10/4 half-track mounting a 2cm Flak 30 during operations on the Eastern Front. The crew all wear the universally supplied Zeltbahn shelter quarters to protect themselves from the elements. Note the weight of the vehicle painted in white letters beside the driver's compartment.

A 4.7cm PaK Sf auf Panzerkampfwagen I Panzerjäger operating in Russia during the summer of 1941. This vehicle has halted on a road and a soldier can be seen conversing with the driver through the tank letterbox side hatch.

A half-track Sd.Kfz.10/4 complete with 2cm Flak 30 has halted along a road. Note the sides of the vehicle are secured for travel and the ammunition bins can be seen fixed to its sides.

A Marder I Panzerjäger Lorraine on what appears to be a testing ground. The Marder I was used to equip smaller anti-tank companies and mainly reinforced infantry and a few panzer divisions' anti-tank battalions.

A Marder II with a shirtless crew during the summer of 1942. This tank hunter mounts the Soviet 7.62cm gun. These vehicles were incorporated into anti-tank battalions of both Wehrmacht and Waffen-SS panzer divisions. However, due to the high silhouette and open-top fighting compartment, it made the machine vulnerable to indirect enemy fire. The armour, too, was thin.

A whitewashed Marder II in Russia during winter operations. Despite its vulnerability out in the field, this Panzerjäger was a very effective weapon, especially during defensive roles, where it was employed increasingly.

A Marder III can be seen rolling along a road complete with trailer. An Sd.Kfz.251 armoured personnel carrier can be seen further along the road. Note the commanding officers watching the vehicles pass.

Inside a fighting compartment of a Marder III.

A Marder III, complete with trailer, advances through a town. The gun traverse of this Panzerjäger was 21 degrees right and left. The vehicle is painted a solid colour, possibly dark grey. Canvas sheeting is protecting the fighting compartment from the elements.

A Nashorn advances along a typical Russian road that has been turned into mire following a heavy downpour of rain. In order to prevent dirt and muddy particles entering the gun tube the crew have fitted its canvas cover over the front of the barrel.

A battery of Marder IIs armed with 76.2mm guns cross a wooden bridge during operations on the Eastern Front.

A Dicker Max 10.5cm K18 auf Panzer Selbstfahrlafette IV Ausf. A during operations in Russia. This self-propelled anti-tank vehicle mounted a 10.5cm schwere Kanone 18. It was built to be primarily used against bunkers. However, by the time it made its debut on the Eastern Front in 1941, it was assigned to Panzerjäger-Abteilung 521.

A Dicker Max, which was part of the Schwere Panzerjäger-Abteilung 521, can be seen on a road with a group of soldiers.

In Russia, in the summer of 1941, a Dicker Max with crew belonging to the Schwere Panzerjäger-Abteilung 521 can be seen stationary on a road. Although the 10.5cm gun was powerful it had limited traverse and in order to engage a target the vehicle often had to be turned. This vehicle is painted in solid dark grey (RAL 7021).

(**Opposite, above**) A camouflaged Dicker Max on a road moving to the front during the summer of 1941. The 10.5cm gun proved itself capable of supporting an infantry attack but because of its size a report noted that it lacked proper mobility and created a large dust cloud when firing.

(**Opposite, below**) Panzerjäger 4.7cm PaK auf R35 during operations in 1941. Some 800 R35s were captured by the Germans in 1940 after the fall of France. As a result, a number of them were sent to be converted by the German manufacturer Alkett. By October 1941, over 170 had been converted into the 4.7cm PaK(t) auf Panzerkampfwagen 35R(f) ohne Turm, a 4.7cm tank destroyer, to replace the Panzerjäger I.

(**Above**) The crew of a Wehrmacht Sd.Kfz.10/4 half-track pose for the camera. Some six or seven crew members, including a commander, two gunners and three loaders, operated this anti-flak vehicle. During the invasion of Russia, these vehicles were for the first time organised within the Heer.

Two photographs showing an Sd.Kfz.10/4 half-track. This vehicle saw extensive use during the Second World War. Initially, its main role was as a prime mover for small towed guns, such as the 2cm Flak 30, the 7.5cm le.IG, or the 3.7cm PaK 36 anti-tank gun. It could carry eight troops in addition to towing a gun or trailer. Both of these half-tracks have been converted into self-propelled anti-flak vehicles and mounted with the 2cm Flak 38 gun. They are towing ammunition trailers.

A Panzerjäger 38t 7.62cm PaK 36r Marder III with crew.

A Luftwaffe Sd.Kfz.7/2 Flak half-track sits in an Italian seaport. Three ammunition boxes can be seen sitting on the track guard.

A half-track mounting a 2cm Flak 30 bolted onto the rear of an Sd.Kfz.10/4.

A Waffen-SS Totenkopf Sd.Kfz.10/4 mounting a 2cm Flak gun during its advance through Russia in 1941. This half-track and its ammunition trailer are dark grey (RAL 7021).

A Waffen-SS Sd.Kfz.7/1 half-track mounting a Flak gun. The Sd.Kfz.7 half-track prime mover was usually used to tow artillery and was also the standard prime mover for 8.8cm Flak. On later variants, the cab was provided with light armour.

A Waffen-SS flak crew converse next to their modified artillery tractor during operations on the Eastern Front in 1941.

A Marder III has halted on a muddy tract of open land. Note the battalion's insignia painted on the side of the hull. Attached to the front of the vehicle are six 20-litre fuel cans, which were used for long-distance operations.

A Marder III armed with the 7.5cm PaK gun converted on the chassis of a Pz.Kpfw.38(t). The vehicle has been factory painted a dark yellow (RAL 7028) base colour, over which one or two other colours could be applied by the unit. Late in the war, the most commonly applied summer camouflage colours were dark olive green (RAL 6003) and red brown (RAL 8017). A common alternative colour was olive green (RAL 8002).

A Marder III halted in a field. The vehicle's commander can be seen conversing with infantry. The Marder was often used in an infantry supporting role on the battlefield. With so many Russian 76.2mm guns captured by the Germans, the gun became one of the most numerous in their anti-tank arsenal.

A Marder III armed with the 7.5cm PaK gun. The high profile of these anti-tank vehicles and their limited side and rear armour caused crews a great number of problems and high causalities.

A Marder II concealing itself in undergrowth during operations on the Eastern Front. It appears that the vehicle is undergoing some maintenance.

A view of the fighting compartment of a Marder III Ausf. M variant.

A Marder III advances across a field.

An Sd.Kfz.10/4 during operations on the Eastern Front in 1942. Four crew members are keeping vigilant and are surveying the sky for enemy aircraft.

An Sd.Kfz.251/10 Schützenpanzerwagen 3.7cm PaK. This half-track is mounting a 3.7cm PaK 36 anti-tank gun. Early variants used the whole top half of a PaK 36 with full gun shield, but later, Ausf. C & D used a smaller, half-size gun shield.

An Sd.Kfz.10/4 in combat. The vehicle mounts the Flak 30. The side boards have been lowered in order to either traverse the weapon or allow more work space for the crew.

An Sd.Kfz.8 mounting the 8.8cm Flak 18 (Sf.) during operations in Russia in 1942.

The crew of a Marder II pose for the camera in a field. Due to the ever-increasing demand put on the Panzerwaffe in the first year of the Russia campaign, more and more anti-tank vehicles were required. By the summer of 1942, a group of seventy-two Marder I and IIs were designated to Army Group Centre in Russia and assigned to various infantry and panzer divisions.

Three photographs taken in sequence, showing an Sd.Kfz.10 mounting a Flak gun in operation in Russia, probably in 1942. This vehicle belongs to the Waffen-SS Leibstandarte Adolf Hitler Panzer Division. Note the divisional insignia painted on the rear of the Sd.Ah.51 ammunition trailer.

(**Opposite, above**) This half-track mounted 2cm Flakvierling is prepared for a fire mission. The gunner can be seen surveying both ground and aerial targets.

(**Opposite, below**) A battery of 2cm Flak on half-tracks during a fire mission against an aerial target during operations on the Eastern Front. In order to prepare the gun quickly for action the crew were able to stow their equipment on their vehicle or its ammunition trailer.

(**Above**) A Nashorn has apparently halted inside an Italian village. Note the canvas sheeting covering the crew compartment. The tactical number '211' is painted in black. This vehicles belongs to 2 Company Heavy Panzer Hunter Battalion, and is pictured near Anzio in March 1944.

(**Below**) A half-track towing an 8.8cm Flak gun passes a Nashorn moving along the same muddy road in the opposite direction. The Nashorns were often found in independent Panzerjäger heavy tank battalions and depending on operational needs, were sometimes attached to different army corps.

A Nashorn advances along a road. The high profile of the vehicle made it hard to conceal, but its long-range gun enabled it to fight further distances than other tank destroyers.

Chapter Three

Stopgap Solution (1943–44)

By 1943, the German war machine was forced to continually improvise obsolete or damaged vehicles and convert them into both flak and anti-tank vehicles. In doing so they hoped that the Panzerwaffe could continue to maintain themselves in the field and hopefully wear down the enemy's offensive capacity. What the Germans actually now found themselves doing on the battlefield was fighting a war of attrition against a foe that was steadily growing both on the ground and in the air. German anti-tank and flak units were compelled to try to fill the gaps left by the infantry and hold the front at whatever cost in men and material. Throughout early 1942 and early 1943, self-propelled anti-tank and aircraft units fought well and were regarded as making a significant contribution to the overstretched Panzerwaffe.

During this period of the war there was much innovation in adapting and converting tank chassis and half-tracks. There had been the introduction of the Sd.Kfz.10/5 Flak 38; the Sd.Kfz.7 half-track was also converted into a number of self-propelled anti-aircraft variants using both the 2cm and 3.7cm Flak guns. The Sd.Kfz.7/1 was converted and mounted the powerful 2cm Flakvierling 38 quadruple Flak gun. The Sd.Kfz.7/2 variant was armed with a single 3.7cm Flak 36 anti-aircraft gun. There were also numerous conversions made mounting a single 2cm anti-aircraft gun. Trial vehicles mounting a 5cm Flak 41 were also produced, but these machines proved unreliable and production was consequently halted.

Conversions were also later made to the Sd.Kfz.251 half-tracks. The Sd.Kfz.251/10, which was equipped with the 3.7cm PaK 36 anti-tank gun, was slowly phased out for the Sd.Kfz.251/17 variant. This variant was a medium armoured personnel carrier mounting a Flak 2cm KwK 30 or 38 gun. The weapon was also designed to be used in a dual-purpose role and could fire against both aerial and ground targets.

In spite of the various modifications that were made to increase the survivability of the Germans on the battlefield, through the first half of 1943 the Red Army were slowly outgunning them, and the Luftwaffe air support was almost non-existent in a number of areas of the front. The short summer nights too had caused considerable problems for the Panzerwaffe, for they only had a few hours of darkness in which to conceal their night marches and construction of field fortifications. Ultimately, in the summer of that year, the Panzerwaffe was ill-prepared to launch a massive offensive in the East, even with considerable support of panzers and new self-propelled anti-aircraft and anti-tank guns. Yet, despite growing problems, Hitler was to gamble his armour in Russia in a large-scale offensive known as the Battle of Kursk.

One machine that was to make its first appearance for this massive German offensive was the new Panzerjäger Tiger (P) 8.8cm PaK 43/2 L/71 Ferdinand/Elefant (Sd.Kfz.184). This monster vehicle was a heavy tank destroyer that was to be used by anti-tank units. Ninety-one of these vehicles were built in 1943 under the name Ferdinand, using tank hulls that had been manufactured for the Tiger I tank. Eighty-nine of these new Ferdinand/Elefant machines were committed to Kursk in July 1943. The vehicle was fitted with a powerful 8.8cm StuK 43/1. The gun had been originally developed as a replacement for the standard 8.8cm Flak gun. It had a much longer barrel than the L/56, and gave the gun a much more potent punch. The Ferdinand/Elefant was primarily used at Kursk to protect the flanks and the rear of advancing armour. They were also to be used with great effect to stem enemy tank assaults and destroy T-34 medium tanks.

Following the lost battle at Kursk, surviving Ferdinand/Elefants continued fighting rearguard actions during the summer of 1943 until they were recalled to be modified and overhauled. The vehicles would not return to the battlefield until early 1944. Modifications of the vehicle included the addition of a ball-mounted MG 34 in the hull front, a new commander's cupola, redesigned armoured engine grates and an application of Zimmerit anti-magnetic mine paste. Eleven of the first completed modified versions were sent to Italy and were issued to the 1st Company of the 653rd Heavy Panzerjäger Battalion in response to the Allied landing at Anzio-Nettuno. The remaining vehicles were sent via train, bound for Tarnopol (now Ternopil) during defensive actions in Ukraine.

In Italy, following the Italian Armistice of 8 September 1943, the Germans captured thousands of Italian vehicles. Many of them were outdated machines and in need of repair. As a result, the Germans proposed to modify the Italian Semovente M43 da 105/25, designated by the Germans as the Beute Sturmgeschütz M43 mit 10.5cm KwK L/25 853. These vehicles were captured assault M43 guns with 105mm L/25 anti-aircraft cannon. Following their modification, a prototype was assigned to a training school in northern Italy that trained with Panzerjäger and German-equipped Italian tank destroyer squads. Later, these vehicles were operational and saw action with heavy anti-tank gun platoons. They were capable of dealing with most Allied armour but their service was short and the numbers modified made no tactical difference on the battlefield.

On the Eastern Front, the winter of 1943 opened up with an exasperating series of deliberations for the Panzerwaffe. Much of its concern was preventing the overwhelming might of the Red Army with what little it had at its disposal. During the winter, all units on the Eastern Front averaged 2,000 tanks, of which, only 800 were regarded as combat ready at any one time. It was indeed a very small force for such a large front to cover. In order to try to compensate for this shortfall, the Panzerwaffe was increasingly dependent on the self-propelled anti-tank and flak units. As a result of this growing reliance, vehicles were being increasingly modified, adapted and converted for the battlefield to deal with the overwhelming enemy threat. By the end of 1943, there was a drastic requirement for more powerful tank destroyers due to massive tank losses and a huge shortfall in production capabilities. The Germans were therefore forced to introduce a new range of Jagdpanzer that could deliver a heavy punch to the enemy and be very cost-effective to manufacture. The Sturmgeschütz III (StuG III) assault gun, for instance, had shown the Germans how well that vehicle had performed on the battlefield with its lethal 7.5cm StuK 40 L/48 gun. It had been designed purely to support infantry and was financially viable to produce, unlike heavier tanks such as the Tiger and Panther. In fact, by late 1943, more StuG IIIs than tanks were built in order to speed up production lines. As a result, more and more Panzerjäger units, comprising various divisions, also received their own assault gun units. This was undertaken in order to compensate for the lack of tanks and many of the panzer and Panzergrenadier divisions began absorbing lots of these artillery assault gun units into the panzer troops and utilising them in anti-tank roles. Technically, the StuG III was not a Jagdpanzer, but desperation meant that these vehicles would be used as effective tank killers. In late 1943 and early 1944, the assault guns were increasingly equipping the Panzerjäger companies. The Sturmgeschütz continued to fight very effectively, in spite of overwhelming resistance from the enemy.

Throughout January and February 1944, the winter did nothing to impede the Soviet might from grinding further west. During February, the organisation of a Sturmgeschütz assault gun battery was changed to consist of four platoons, one of which had three 10.5cm assault howitzer 42 units, and three platoons equipped with three 7.5cm assault cannon 40 units. Together with two assault guns of the battery leader, there were fourteen vehicles in each battery.

The alteration was supposed to make the gun batteries more effective and lethal on the battlefield. Whilst it increased the firepower and anti-tank capability, crews still found they were numerically outnumbered. As a direct consequence, they suffered heavy losses.

Yet, despite the severe losses, by the time the spring thaw arrived in March and early April 1944, there was a genuine feeling of motivation within the ranks of the Panzerwaffe. There was renewed determination to keep the Red Army out of the Homeland. In addition, confidence was further bolstered by the efforts of the armaments industry as they began producing many new vehicles for the Eastern Front. During 1944, the Panzerwaffe were better supplied with equipment than at any other time on the Eastern Front, thanks to the armaments industry. In total, some 20,000 fighting vehicles, including 8,328 medium and heavy tanks, 5,751 assault guns, 3,617 tank destroyers and 1,246 self-propelled artillery carriages of various types reached the Eastern Front. Included in these new arrivals were the second generation of tank destroyers, the Jagdpanzer IV, followed by the Jagdpanzer 38 and then the Jadgpanther and Jagdtiger. Tank destroyers and assault guns now actually outnumbered the tanks, which was confirmation of the Panzerwaffe's obligation to performing a defensive role against overwhelming opposition. All of these vehicles would have to be irrevocably stretched along a very thin Eastern Front, with many of them rarely reaching the proper operating level.

A Waffen-SS Sd.Kfz.10/4 mounting a Flak gun during operations in Russia in 1943.

Repairs are being made to an Sd.Kfz.7/1 medium half-track mounting the 2cm Flakvierling Flak 38 quad anti-aircraft gun. The Flakvierling mounted four 2cm Flak 38 guns and had a maximum rate of fire of 1,800 rounds per minute. Though intended for anti-aircraft use, it was also effective against ground targets. The guns could be traversed 360 degrees by hand and elevated from –10 to +100 degrees.

A crew member wearing the standard Wehrmacht greatcoat stands on the fighting platform of an Sd.Kfz.7/1 medium half-track mounting the 2cm Flakvierling Flak 38 quad anti-aircraft gun. The crew comprised ten men including the commander, eight gunners and a driver. The vehicle carried 600 rounds of 2cm ammunition. An additional 1,800 rounds were stored in a special single-axle trailer.

With winter camouflage paint, an Sd.Kfz.10/4 can be seen halted on a road with crew posing for the camera.

An Sd.Kfz.7/1 medium half-track mounting the 2cm Flakvierling Flak 38 quad anti-aircraft gun. This was a specially modified version of the 8-ton capacity Sd.Kfz.7 half-track prime mover. The low unarmoured steel side boards have been lowered in preparation for operation. Note the white wavy lines painted over the gun shield by the crew in order to break up the distinctive shape of the vehicle in the snow. The first 100 of these vehicles were produced from April 1940 to mid-1941 and continued at a rate of ten per month until August 1942. Production was then increased and 750 to 800 vehicles were produced by December 1944.

A 2cm Flak 30 Sd.Kfz.10/4 half-track crew prepare to enter a Russian village with caution. Note two of the crewmen armed with the MP40 machine gun and two Stg-24 stick grenades.

A half-track mounting the 2cm Flak 38 gun surveys the sky for enemy aircraft. Note the MG 34 machine-gun ammunition boxes resting on the lowered side boards and it includes a steel carrier comprising two fifty-round machine-gun drums.

A well-camouflaged Sd.Kfz.10/5 half-track mounting the 2cm Flak 38 halts on a road as an Sd.Kfz.251/1 armoured personnel carrier passes, carrying Panzergrenadiers.

During operations in the snow, an uncamouflaged Sd.Kfz.10 positions its gun against possible ground targets.

A fully laden Sd.Kfz.10.4 advances through a snow-covered village on the Eastern Front.

During operations on the Eastern Front, officers can be seen with the crew of an Sd.Kfz.251/10.

On the advance with troops following in the rear is an Sd.Kfz.251/10 equipped with the 3.7cm Pak 36 anti-tank gun.

A mid to late image showing an Sd.Kfz.10/10 Schützenpanzerwagen (3.7cm PaK). The half-track was equipped with a 3.7cm PaK 36 anti-tank gun mount.

A photograph most likely taken on the Eastern Front in 1942. It shows an Sd.Kfz.10/10 Schützenpanzerwagen (3.7cm PaK). These vehicles were issued to platoon leaders as a fire support vehicle.

Six photographs showing the Sturmgeschütz III (StuG) mounting the 7.5cm StuK 40 L/48 during operations in Russia. When building the StuG, tacticians decided that in order for the artillery to play a prominent part in the new mobile warfare and remain operating in close contact to the battle zone, they needed a highly mobile artillery piece. The result was the Sturmgeschütz assault gun. This vehicle was intended to keep pace with the mechanised infantry, afford the gunners a degree of armoured protection, and provide support on the battlefield at short notice. An armoured tracked mobile gun was thought to be the best solution to the problem, which could provide close artillery support to the advancing infantry. Whilst the assault guns remained in close contact with the infantry and were unhindered by the rapid drive, by 1942 and 1943 they were slowly deprived of local fire support from the panzers. As a direct result, the Sturmgeschütz became increasingly embroiled in heavy fighting and were continually called upon for offensive and defensive fire support, which consequently caused a series of high losses in a number of units. Gradually, units were compelled to operate increasingly in an anti-tank role. Although technically not a Panzerjäger, the StuG had excellent tank-killing potential and fought well in both offensive and defensive roles. However, the increased use of the StuG as an anti-tank weapon began depriving the infantry of the fire support for which the assault gun was originally built.

A crew member scrutinises a map during his drive across the Russian steppes with his upgraded Panzerjäger Tiger (P). Initially, this tank destroyer was known as the Ferdinand, but its name was officially changed to Elefant in February 1944, on Hitler's orders.

A prime mover towing an 8.8cm Flak gun passes a stationary Panzerjäger Tiger (P). These vehicles were primarily built for destroying T-34 tanks, a role that the tank hunter performed very well.

A Nashorn during winter operations in 1943. The vehicle mounted the 8.8cm 43/1 auf Fahrgestell on the chassis of a Pz.Kpfw.III and Pz.Kpfw.IV on the same hybrid chassis as the 15cm Hummel howitzer.

A Nashorn has halted along a track and a dispatch horse rider hands the commander communiqué. This vehicle was introduced in the spring of 1943; it was initially known as the Hornisse (Hornet) and later as the Nashorn (Rhinoceros), of which 494 were built.

(**Above**) Two Nashorns can be seen halted in the snow. The design of the Nashorn was the first attempt by the Germans to mount an 8.8cm anti-tank gun on a self-propelled mount.

(**Opposite**) An interesting photograph showing the crew retracking a Nashorn in the snow. Although the gun it mounted was very powerful, the vehicle was lightly armoured, possessed a high profile and was overweight, resulting in limited cross-country mobility. It was first introduced at Kursk.

(**Below**) A column of whitewashed Nashorns advance along a road, bound for the front.

A Nashorn prepares to move out from its position with supporting infantry. The vehicle has been whitewashed. Its 8.8cm gun is in its lock position. Note the canvas sheeting, which was used to protect the fighting compartment from the elements.

It appears that this Ferdinand Elefant is being resupplied with ammunition from the rear of a support truck during operations on the Eastern Front. This tank hunter weighed a staggering 65 tonnes and was manned by a crew of six.

A crewman is supplying his Ferdinand Elefant through the rear round door with a projectile. Note the Zimmerit anti-magnetic mine paste applied to the vehicle's lower hull.

A Ferdinand Elefant has been unloaded from a specially adapted railway flatbed. One of the most common and practical methods of transporting armour was by rail. Sometimes, whole panzer divisions were moved by train from one part of the battle front to another so the vehicles could quickly be readied for action.

A Ferdinand Elefant is concealed among a group of trees in order to prevent enemy aerial observation. The vehicle's tactical number, '534', is painted in white on the side of is armoured hull. It has an effective pattern of dark olive green (RAL 6003) highlighted with red brown (RAL 8017) and has been painted over the dark yellow (RAL 7028) sand base.

Kübelwagen cars can be seen stationary next to a Ferdinand Elefant. Throughout the later period of the war, this Panzerjäger continued to provide its worth as an invaluable anti-tank weapon. Yet, in spite of the huge losses, in a number of last-ditch battles it showed its true capabilities as a tank killer.

The crew of a Ferdinand Elefant pose for the obligatory photo shot, with two members sitting on the vehicle's 8.8cm cannon.

Frontal view of an M42 da 7518 (left) and the prototype of the M43 da 10525 (right) at the Ansaldo-Fossati plant in Genoa.

A 12.8cm Selbstfahrlafette auf VK 30.01(H) 'Sturer Emil', or 'Stubborn Emil', halted in southern Russia. This vehicle was purposely built as a self-propelled anti-fortification gun. It was armed with a 12.8cm Kanone 40 L/61 gun, which was based on the 12.8cm Flak 40. This gun could traverse 7 degrees to each side, elevate 10 degrees and depress –15 degrees. It carried fifteen rounds for the main gun.

A 12.8cm Selbstfahrlafette auf VK 30.01(H) 'Sturer Emil' advances towards the battlefield, probably in the summer of 1942. Only two vehicles were built and nicknamed after the story book characters Max and Moritz. *Max* was probably lost in battle, while *Moritz* was captured at Stalingrad in January 1943.

A crewman wearing a familiar black panzer uniform worn by self-propelled anti-tank battalions poses for the camera on board his Marder II. This vehicle has been heavily camouflaged in order to break up its distinctive shape.

Chapter Four

Second Generation (1944–45)

With the ever-increasing need for firepower, the Germans began effectively designing stronger second-generation anti-tank and anti-aircraft vehicles capable of knocking out heavier enemy armour. By 1944, the need for mobile and effective tank killers became more urgent than ever before. Due to production issues, the Germans were often compelled to reuse knocked-out and recovered tank chassis. This time, more potent anti-tank guns would be universally used, including the 8.8cm PaK 43 and 7.5cm PaK 40 anti-tank guns. The modified 7.5cm PaK 40 had been very successful with the Marder II and III. But as these machines were phased out, various second-generation machines were successfully adapted with the 7.5cm gun. The 7.5cm PaK 40 auf Raupenschlepper Ost (RSO), for instance, was customised into a tank destroyer. This tractor vehicle had been initially built to tow ordnance and supplies to the front. Some 27,000 of them had been built by 1945. The first deployment of this new anti-tank machine was in Army Group Centre in January 1944. Another vehicle to be adapted with the 7.5cm gun was the Sd.Kfz.251/22 half-track, which was designated as the 7.5cm PaK40 L/46 auf mittlerem Schützenpanzerwagen. Although the gun was oversized for the fighting compartment, it was still effective on the battlefield.

Other vehicles were also adapted with the 7.5cm gun, including reconnaissance vehicles such as the Sd.Kfz.234/3 and Sd.Kfz.234/4. However, these were not technically tank hunters. The creation of the first dedicated Panzerjäger was the Jagdpanzer IV (Sd.Kfz.162). The vehicle was intended to be a replacement for the Sturmgeschütz III and its construction used a modified Pz.Kpfw.IV Ausf. H chassis complete with 80mm sloped armoured plates. In order to make production more efficient and less time-consuming, the superstructure was made from large interlocking plates that were simply welded together. The machine's main armament was the 7.5cm PaK 42 L/70. Production of the Jagdpanzer IV began in late 1943. There were plans to phase out the Pz.Kpfw.IV and entirely concentrate on manufacturing the Jagdpanzer IV. The Jagdpanzer IV entered service in the first part of 1944 and was used to equip the anti-tank battalions of the Panzer or Panzergrenadier battalions. The vehicles saw extensive action on both the Western Front and the Eastern Front. It also operated in Italy, but in small numbers.

With the decision to swap production of the Pz.Kpfw.IV and concentrate on the Jagdpanzer IV, the Germans made a modified version known as a Jagdpanzer IV/70 (V). This vehicle was an improved version armed with the 7.5cm L/70 gun. Amazingly, by the end of the war some 1,000 of these machines had been produced. In fact, the Jagdpanzer IV saw its designation name change through the course of the year. During 1944, the designation name of the vehicle changed a number of times, and it was given the final designation as the Jagdpanzer IV/70 (A) from November 1944. The letter 'A' stood for the Alkett company, which developed the vehicle. The chassis of the tank hunter was adapted from the Pz.Kpfw.IV Ausf. J.

While the Jagdpanzer IV was being manufactured and sent to the Eastern Front, other second-generation tank destroyers were being built, such as the Jagdtiger (Sd.Kfz.186). The Jagdtiger was officially designated Panzerjäger Tiger Ausf. B, which was built on a modified chassis of a Tiger II tank. The design of the vehicle was similar to other second-generation Jagdpanzers that were entering service in 1944. It weighed a staggering 71 tonnes and was armed with a 12.8cm PaK 44 L/55 gun. Its anti-tank gun had a medium range performance similar to the 8.8cm PaK 43, but the 44 had better long-range action and plenty of punch. The armour casemate was 250mm thick, with the hull 150mm and the rear and sides 80mm. It had a crew of six, comprising the commander, gunner, loader, assistant loader, driver and assistant driver. Around 150 of these vehicles were initially ordered, but only about eighty of them were manufactured, between July 1944 and April 1945. Only two heavy anti-tank battalions were equipped with the Jagdtiger, with the first vehicles reaching their units in September 1944. Losses were considerably high due to mechanical breakdown, insufficient training of crews and lack of fuel. In spite of its size and thick armour plating, it was susceptible to American bazookas.

While the Jagdtiger was being developed and built, another tank hunter was prepared to enter service. Known as the Jagdpanther Sd.Kfz.173, it mounted the 8.8cm PaK 43/3 L/71 anti-tank gun. Once again, this second-generation vehicle was a non-turreted tank destroyer with sloped glacis plate and hull sides that extended up into an integral fixed casemate. There were two variants built: the G1 1944 comprised a welded main gun mantlet on a modified Panther Ausf. A engine deck; the G2 variant used the Panther Ausf. G engine deck, which boasted a larger gun mantlet bolted externally.

A total of 413 Jagdpanthers were manufactured from January 1944 and entered service in March 1944 on the Eastern Front in heavy anti-tank battalions; they fought in Russia and then encountered Allied soldiers on the

Western Front in Normandy, but only in small numbers. They were also deployed for action in larger numbers for the Ardennes Offensive.

Another Jagdpanzer to be built during the same period as the Jagdpanther was the Jagdpanzer 38 tank hunter. It was modified on the old chassis of the Pz.Kpfw.38(t) and the open-topped Marder III. It mounted a powerful high-velocity 7.5cm PaK 39 L/48 gun and was a very cost-effective, second-generation tank killer compared to the Jagdtiger and Jagdpanther. Some 2,827 of these vehicles were produced.

The Jagdpanzer 38 equipped the tank destroyer battalions of the infantry divisions and gave them a vehicle that had relatively good mobile anti-tank capability. They first saw active service on the Eastern Front in July 1944. Two companies of the Jagdpanzer 38 were later sent to the Arnhem sector in September 1944. Some 295 of the vehicles were used in the Ardennes Offensive with some success, in spite high losses.

While the second-generation Jagdpanzers were making their debut in 1944, the Germans were also aware of the significant requirement to support troops not only on the ground but also in the air. By 1944, the Luftwaffe was almost nonexistent and the skies were dominated by both Russian and Allied aircraft. As a result, a concept was invented in the summer of 1944 to remove the turret of a Pz.Kpfw.IV and replace it with an open-top, nine-sided turret that mounted a powerful 2cm Flakvierling 38, which was a quadruple mount of 2cm cannon. It was designated as the Flakpanzer IV Wirbelwind (Whirlwind). The vehicle had a powerful turret of four barrels capable of firing 2cm shells at a high rate. It was principally successful against ground targets, especially attacking lightly armoured enemy trucks and cars. Infantry too were particularly vulnerable. Between 87 and 105 Wirbelwind were converted on the chassis from repaired Pz.Kpfw.IVs. Although the Flakpanzer was successful on the ground, against air targets it lacked range and was often ineffective at knocking out aircraft. As a consequence, it was replaced with the Flakpanzer IV Ostwind (East Wind), which was equipped with a single 3.7cm Flak 43.

In spite the various self-propelled anti-tank and anti-aircraft vehicles that fought both on the Western and the Eastern Front, by late 1944 nothing could mask the fact that the Flakpanzers and Jagdpanzers were a stopgap solution aimed at preventing the inevitable defeat of the German war machine. By late January 1945, the Russians were making deep and wide-sweeping penetrations against hard-pressed German armoured formations. The Russian offensive was delivered with so much weight and fury that Red Army troops were soon in Poland. The frozen ground ensured rapid movement for the Russian tank crews, but in some areas these massive advances were halted for a time by the skilful dispositions of Panzer and Panzerjäger units. By this time, the action strength of the Panzerjäger and Flakpanzer units had fallen to an all-time low. Losses of equipment had also markedly increased in the course of the retreat combat. Often, the assault gun crews would abandon their vehicles when they ran out of fuel and were seen regularly running on foot or hitching a lift on board a variety of other vehicles.

In early 1945, armoured production figures dropped and as a result of this decline, units no longer had any reserves on which to rely. When defensive fighting began in Germany there was a severe lack of fuel and spare parts, as well as a lack of trained crews. When parts of the front caved in, the remaining Panzerjäger units were often forced to destroy their equipment so nothing was left for the conquering enemy. Thus, the Germans no longer had the manpower, war plant or transportation to accomplish a proper build-up of forces. Commanders could do little to compensate for the deficiencies, and in many sectors of the front they did not have any coherent planning in the event of any defensive position being lost.

During the last days of the war most of the remaining assault Flak and PaK gun units continued to fight as a unit until they destroyed their equipment and surrendered. At the time of surrender, the combined strength of the entire Panzerwaffe was 2,023 tanks, 738 assault guns and 159 Flakpanzers. Surprisingly, this was the same strength that was used to attack Russia in 1941. But the size of the German Army in 1945 was not the same; it was far too inadequate in strength for any type of task.

Two whitewashed Nashorn tank destroyers belonging to the 519th Schwere Panzerjäger-Abteilung in Russia, near Witebsk, in the winter of 1944.

An Sd.Kfz.7/1 Flak gun belonging to the 27th SS Volunteer Division Langemarck during operations in March 1944. This vehicle was more than likely attached to the SS-Panzerjäger Battalion 27. The division fought alongside Das Reich near Zhitomir (Zhytomyr), suffering massive casualties after being encircled.

An Sd.Kfz.10/4 advances across terrain somewhere in southern Russia. Foliage has been applied to the ammunition trailer. The rail sides of the vehicle are down in order for the crew to go into action at a moment's notice.

A Jagdpanther during a field exercise in France in 1944. The Jagdpanther mounted the powerful 8.8cm PaK 43/3 L/71 anti-tank gun, similar to the main gun of the Tiger II, with the armour and suspension of the Panther chassis. Production of these new tank hunters began in January 1944.

A Jagdpanther belonging to Schwere Panzerjäger-Abteilung 654. This particular anti-tank battalion was deployed in France and saw some fighting during the Battle of Normandy. Twelve vehicles saw action.

A Jagdpanther crewman can be seen standing next to his tank hunter during operations in France in 1944.

A Ferdinand Elefant being prepared for action on the Eastern Front. One of the crewmen appears to be releasing the locking bar for the 8.8cm cannon. Although Panzerjäger commanders were fully aware of the fruitless attempts by its units to establish permanent lines of defence, the crews followed instructions implicitly in a number of areas to halt the Soviet drive. Again and again, these vehicles fought to the grim end.

A Marder I (Sd.Kfz.135) pictured during an exercise in France. This Lorraine Schlepper-based Marder continued to serve on both the Eastern Front and the Western Front, mainly between 1942 and early 1945. These Panzerjäger would see extensive action during the Normandy campaign in June 1944.

A Marder III halted on a road so that the crew can apply foliage to the vehicle in order to camouflage the Panzerjäger. By late 1944, it became increasingly obvious that the assault gun, although built in huge numbers, was no longer as effective on the battlefield. Whilst the second-generation tank hunter was still regarded as a lethal weapon, the Russians had already developed newer and larger anti-tank killers of their own, with greater armoured protection and better firepower. As a result, the Russians continued pushing forward.

An abandoned Jagdpanzer IV/Sd.Kfz.162 in France in 1944. This vehicle was based on the Pz.Kpfw.IV chassis and built in three variants. It served in the anti-tank units of panzer and SS panzer divisions, where it saw operations on the Western Front in Normandy in June 1944 and during the Ardennes Offensive in December 1944. It also saw fighting on the Eastern Front. Its low profile, lethal gun and good armour protection meant that it was embroiled in a number of successful engagements.

Four popular photographs taken in sequence, showing the 7.5cm PaK 40 auf Sf. Lorraine Schlepper Marder I being unloaded from a special flatbed rail car in France in 1944. This effective and lethal 7.5cm anti-tank gun could destroy most Allied tanks at long ranges. The majority of these tank hunters were stationed in France, and it was often standard practice for these vehicles to be relocated to another front, mainly the Eastern Front.

A converted Sd.Kfz.7/1 mounting the powerful 2cm Flakvierling 38 quadruple Flak gun being prepared for a fire mission.

Another photograph of a converted Sd.Kfz.7/1, which is well-concealed in a forest in northern Russia.

During the late war period, the Germans increasingly began to modify various vehicles that could mount PaK or Flak guns. This photograph shows a Flak gun mounted on a four-wheeled vehicle defending a position in 1944.

A Ferdinand Elefant belonging to Kampfgruppe Ulbricht during operations in Italy in the summer of 1944.

Saplings have been applied to this Nashorn during operations in Italy in 1944. For additional concealment, the crew have parked the vehicle next to a building. Initially, these Panzerjäger could provide adequate support and increase the offensive capabilities of both Wehrmacht and Waffen-SS units. However, by 1944, the majority of these vehicles were used extensively for defensive purposes and as a result, losses were high.

A well-camouflaged Nashorn operating in Italy in 1944. In spite of successful engagements against Allied vehicles, the Nashorn did not operate very well in the hilly terrain of Italy. The terrain factor also played a pivotal part in curtailing its ability for long-range firing.

Part of Panzerjäger battalion and a group of Nashorns can be seen near Anzio in 1944. Nashorns were found in dependent heavy anti-tank battalions and were also grouped into independent battalions, which comprised some forty-five vehicles, divided into three companies with fourteen Nashorns in each.

A camouflaged 2cm Flakvierling Sd.Kfz.7 half-track. The side boards are secured and locked; when in action, they were normally lowered to provide crew space for operation. The gun's high profile served it well against both air and ground targets, although it was quite vulnerable on the battlefield in the latter role.

A Jagdpanther attached to the 116 Panzer Division in the town of Lünen in March 1945.

Two crew members pose for the camera in front of their camouflaged Jagdpanzer 38 Sd.Kfz.138/2. It was originally designated as the Leichte Panzerjäger 38(t), but commonly known after the war as the Hetzer.

A Jagdpanzer 38 Sd.Kfz.138/2 negotiating its drive through a small village either in Poland or Russia. These second-generation tank destroyers were mass produced in 1944 and first entered service in July of that year. They would be later assigned to infantry, Panzergrenadier and Volksgrenadier divisions. Some 2,800 were produced.

(**Above**) A popular image showing the Flakpanzer IV Wirbelwind, or Whirlwind, which was a self-propelled anti-aircraft gun based on the chassis of a Pz.Kpfw.IV. To modify the vehicle the Pz.Kpfw.IV turret was removed and replaced with an open top, and a nine-sided turret mounted a 2cm Flakvierling 38, a quadruple mount of 2cm cannon. Around 100 of these Flak machines were produced. They were all incorporated into special anti-tank platoons and equipped panzer divisions of both the Wehrmacht and Waffen-SS. They fought on both the Western Front and the Eastern Front.

(**Opposite, above**) A 3.7cm Flak auf Fahrgestell Panzerkampfwagen IV (Sf.) (Sd.Kfz.161/3), nicknamed Möbelwagen, or 'moving van'. The Möbelwagen was built on the chassis of a Pz.Kpfw.IV chassis and was fitted with an open-top superstructure with the mounted 3.7cm Flak 43 gun. Protecting the gun and crew was a four-hinged 2cm armoured plate, which could also be lowered to allow the gun to be fired against ground targets. This second-generation Flakpanzer was another stopgap solution and it served the anti-aircraft platoons of the panzer divisions on the Western Front. Only 240 were ever produced.

(**Opposite, below**) The Möbelwagen prototype built in 1943. This vehicle is armed with a 2cm quadruple anti-aircraft gun and was the first German anti-aircraft tank based on the Pz.Kpfw.IV hull. This variant was later enhanced and modified with a 3.7cm Flak gun for operations.

Two photographs show captured 7.5cm PaK 40 auf Raupenschlepper Ost (RSO). The RSO was a fully tracked tractor, built to supply Wehrmacht fighting units on the Eastern Front if the terrain was difficult or the weather hampered movement. There were three variants built and this vehicle, known as the RSO/2 or RSO/PaK40, mounted a powerful 7.5cm PaK 40 gun.

Interesting photographs showing two Leichte Einheit Waffenträger (Light Unit Weapon Carrier) 38(D) Ardelt with mounted 8.8cm PaK43/2 L/71. This vehicle was developed during the last year of the war and mounted an 8.8cm PaK gun on the chassis of an old Pz.Kpfw.38(t). Only a small quantity of these vehicles saw action.

A captured Jagdtiger belonging to the Schwere Panzerjäger-Abteilung 653 on the Western Front at Steinweiler Pfalz in 1945. This monster vehicle can be seen on a flat bedrail car and because of its sheer size, parts of its tracks hang over the sides.

An abandoned Jagdtiger belonging to the Schwere Panzerjäger-Abteilung 653. This battalion fought the US Army in March and April 1945 in the area south of Mannheim, from Neustadt an der Weinstrasse to Heidelberg. However, due to strong enemy advances, 653 retreated to southern Bavaria, towards Austria. Although the vehicle was powerful, it was cumbersome and suffered mechanical breakdowns, and never fielded sufficient numbers to avert the deteriorating military situation. As a result, many crews simply abandoned them when they developed mechanical problems or ran out of fuel.

A knocked-out, late production run Sd.Kfz.173 Jagdpanther Ausf. G1 on the Western Front in 1945. This Jagdpanther G1 was a dedicated tank destroyer based on the chassis of the Panther Ausf. A, and was armed with the formidable 8.8cm PaK 43 anti-tank gun. However, like all second-generation tank hunters, it was too little, too late. With only 415 Jagdpanthers produced by the end of the war, there were too few numbers to make any difference to the outcome.

Two abandoned Jagdpanzer IV/70s near Oberpleis, near the Rhine River in Germany, in March 1945. By 1945, the action strength of the Panzerjäger units had fallen to an all-time low and losses of equipment had increased markedly as forces further retreated. Often, crews would abandon their vehicles when they ran out of fuel and were seen regularly running on foot or hitching a lift on board other vehicles that were retreating.

(**Above**) A Panzerjäger that has been knocked out of action in Prague in 1945. This vehicle mounted a powerful 7.5cm PaK 39 L/38 gun.

(**Opposite, above**) An abandoned Jagdpanzer IV L70 in the snow, probably in early 1945. During the winter of 1944/5, German armour production figures dropped and as a result of this decline, units no longer had any reserves on which to rely. When defensive fighting began in Germany there was a severe lack of fuel and spare parts, as well as a lack of trained crews. When parts of the front caved in, the remaining self-propelled anti-tank and anti-aircraft units were often forced to destroy their equipment, so nothing was left for the conquering enemy. The Germans no longer had the manpower, war plant or transportation to accomplish a proper build-up of forces. Armoured crews could do little to compensate for the deficiencies, and in many sectors of the front they did not have any coherent planning in the event of any defensive position being lost.

(**Below**) A Jagdpanzer IV / Sd.Kfz.162 on the Western Front. Civilians pass the knocked-out vehicle among the ruins of a French village. During the last days of the war most of the remaining self-propelled anti-tank and anti-aircraft guns continued to fight as a unit until they destroyed their equipment and surrendered. At the time of surrender, the combined strength of the entire Panzerwaffe comprised 2,023 tanks, 738 assault guns and 159 Flakpanzers. Surprisingly, this was the same strength that was used to attack Russia in 1941. But the size of the German Army in 1945 was not the same; it was far too inadequate in strength for any type of task. Although the war had ended, these vehicles still existed, but not as the offensive weapon they were in the early blitzkrieg years.

Appendix

Jagdpanzer and Flakpanzer Variants

Self-propelled Tank Destroyers (Jagdpanzer)

10.5cm K gepanzerte Selbstfahrlafette 'Dicker Max'
4.7cm PaK(t) (Sf.) auf Fahrgestell Panzerkampfwagen 35R 731(f)
4.7cm PaK(t) (Sf.) auf Panzerkampfwagen I (Sd.Kfz.101) ohne Turm 'Panzerjäger I'
7.5cm PaK 40 auf Raupenschlepper Ost (RSO)
7.62cm F.K. 36(r) auf gepanzerte Selbstfahrlafette Sd.Kfz.6/3
Marder I
Marder II
Marder III
8.8cm PaK 43/1 auf Fahrgestell Panzerkampfwagen III und IV (Sf.) Nashorn (Sd.Kfz.164)
Jagdpanther (Sd.Kfz.173) – March 1944
Jagdpanzer 38 (Hetzer) – early 1944
Jagdpanzer IV (Sd.Kfz.162) – December 1943
Jagdtiger (Sd.Kfz.186) – March 1944
Panzer IV/70(A) – September 1944
Panzer IV/70(V) – late 1944
Panzerjäger Tiger (P) 8.8cm PaK 43/2 L/71 Ferdinand/Elefant (Sd.Kfz.184)
Semovente M43 da 75/46 / Beute Sturmgeschütz M43 mit 7.5cm KwK L/46 852(i) – September 1943

Self-propelled Anti-aircraft Guns (Flakpanzer)

Sd.Kfz.10/4 and 5 2cm Flak 30 – 1940
Sd.Kfz.10/5 Flak 38 – from 1942
Sd.Kfz.7/1
Sd.Kfz.251/17
Flakpanzer 38(t) – 1940
Flakpanzer IV Ostwind – 1944
Flakpanzer IV, Wirbelwind

2cm Flak 30/38 (Sf.) auf gepanzerten Fahrgestell leichte Zugkraftwagen 1-ton (Sd.Kfz.10/4 and Sd.Kfz.10/5)

2cm Flak 38 (Sf.) auf Panzerkampfwagen I Ausf. A Flakpanzer I

3.7cm Flak 43 in Keksdose-Turm auf Panzerkampfwagen III Fahrgestell

Flakpanzer IV (2cm Flakvierling 38) Wirbelwind

Flakpanzer IV (3.7cm Flak 43) Möbelwagen (Sd.Kfz.163/3)

Flakpanzer IV (3.7cm Flak 43) Ostwind

Panzerkampfwagen 38 für 2cm Flak 38 (Sd.Kfz.140) Ausf. L Flakpanzer 38(t)

Schulfahrzeug 1-5b. Serie/La.S. mit MG 34/42 Zwillingssockel 36

Schwere Geländegängiger Lastkraftwagen 4.5t Mercedes-Benz L4500A als Flakwagen

Sd.Kfz.7/1

Notes

Notes

Notes

Notes